THE BOOK OF
FAVOURITE
WORDS

THE BOOK OF
FAVOURITE
WORDS

BLOOMSBURY

First published in 2001 by
Bloomsbury Publishing Plc
38 Soho Square
London W1D 3HB

www.bloomsburymagazine.com

Copyright © 2001 Bloomsbury Publishing Plc

10 9 8 7 6 5 4 3 2 1

A CIP record for this book is available from
the British Library

ISBN 0 7475 5235 5

Designed by Nigel Partridge
Printed and bound in Great Britain by
Clays Ltd, St Ives Plc

Contents

Introduction

Words are described by Kipling as 'the most powerful drug used by mankind.' Many of us may not value the language we use on a daily basis to such an extent, or even give it a second thought, but there is no doubt that words are a vital and creative part of our lives.

When Bob Geldof in his capacity as trustee of The Word – London's literary festival – and Bloomsbury, therefore, set out to discover the nation's favourite word, we started people thinking about language. We set no criteria for selection. It was entirely up to the voters why they felt passionate about a particular group of syllables. We asked celebrities and called on newspapers and websites to help, and 15,000 people volunteered an opinion.

The words were chosen for all manner of reasons. One respondent explained his own criteria: 'Some words I like because of the way they sound when I say them out loud – *crass, pithy, ooze, juxtapose*. Some elicit an actual memory – *sleep, fire, dad*. My favourite words combine sound, emotion, meaning and the pleasure of creation and usage – *mumford, boggle, dartley, grampadappley'*.

Sound, meaning, emotion, invention and creativity. In Lewis Carroll's *Through the Looking Glass*, Humpty Dumpty says 'When I use a word … it means just what I choose it to mean – neither more nor less.' While we may or may not agree with him, this selection of the nation's favourites offers many new and inventive perspectives on words.

The Nation's Favourite Word

The poll to find The Nation's Favourite Word took place over the summer of 2000, in connection with the literary festival The Word.

Serendipity turned out to be the word we loved the most, a word rich in resonance:

Serendipity *n.* a natural gift for making useful discoveries quite by accident [Mid-18thC (but rare before the 20thC). From *The Three Princes of Serendip,* an originally Persian story about three princes who had this ability; 'Serendip' is supposedly a former name of Sri Lanka.]

(ENCARTA WORLD ENGLISH DICTIONARY)

The other words that made the top ten appear below:

Serendipity
Quidditch
Love
Peace / Why
Onomatopoeia

Hope
Faith
Football / Muggle / Hello / Family
Compassion / Home / F**k / Bollocks
Jesus / Money

In this book you will find a further selection of the favourite words of actors, writers, musicians and others polled, as well as a number of words submitted by the general public.

angelica

My favourite word is Angelica. It's the word I use most and hope it's the last word I breathe, so I will be well accompanied into death.
(Angelica is his wife's name)

Ariel Dorfman
(playwright)

apricot

Apricot because it sounds round and fruity and full of sunshine. A happy word.

J.M. Kemp
Cheadle

balls

Balls. There are cricket balls, rugby balls, street lighting in the shape of a set of balls. My one and only swear word is BALLS.

Mary Brown
Bristol

because

Because is my favourite word ... because it is!

Ross Burton
age 14, Taunton

because *conj.* for the reason that follows [14thC. From the phrase *by cause* 'for the reason (that)', which was modelled on Old French *par chance*.]

(ENCARTA WORLD ENGLISH DICTIONARY)

bed

My favourite word is bed –
everything I enjoy I do there. I
watch TV, I sleep, I eat chocolate
and I rest!!

Maggie Barrowman
via email

Beelzebub

My favourite word is Beelzebub
– a pretty word with a sting in
the meaning.

Neal Hounsell
London (Islington)

befuddled

Befuddled: Just sounds damn good and describes my frequent state of mind.

Patrick Evans
Kerry, Ireland, via email

betumble

A rare word which I only know in one context, Thomas Hardy's poem 'Weathers': 'This is the weather the cuckoo likes/ And so do I/ When showers betumble the chestnut spikes/ And nestlings fly'… A rare word returning to my mind with force each spring!

H.E. Payne
Southwell

bizarre

Bizarre is my favourite word
because it sums up today's world
in the strange way we live by
computers and technology and
anything goes attitude. It's so
bizarre.

J. Yardley
Watford

brilliant

I have to nominate brilliant as
Britain's favourite word. Ninety
per cent of users are not aware
of the proper definition of the
word but that does not stop
them using it – incorrectly!

Anon

brouhaha

Brouhaha – because it's a bit like
a herfuffle!

Claire Wearn
via email

brownies

I think I'll pick brownies as my favourite word – I can never hear the word 'brownies' without a surge of joy going through me because I always say 'yes' to them and always eat them. If this is too flip, then I think I'll go for Dordogne, which is just so great to say – and makes your mouth feel rather like you're chewing a lovely brownie.

Richard Curtis
(writer and producer)

bugaboo

Well, it's on the first page of *Salt and Saffron* (along with the reason bi-lingual Pakistanis love the word) so, yes, I'll stick with bugaboo.

Kamila Shamsie
(author)

champion

Champion. I grew up in the 40s and 50s and at that time money was not too good. Through those times we would say to dad 'How's everything?' and he would stroke the back of our heads and say, 'Everything is champion!'

J. Quarmby
Middleton

chocabloc

I am at one with my girlfriend's nine-year-old daughter. The best word in the English language is chocabloc.

Phil Rees
via email

chortle

My favourite word is chortle – a mixture of snort and chuckle, invented by Lewis Carroll in *Alice Through the Looking Glass*.

Faye Carney
via email

clock

Clock because it conjures up a feeling of comfort, warmth and chunkiness. It sounds rounded.

Kim Sillitoe
Wendover

codswallop

Our favourite word is codswallop. This is a good all-purpose alternative to bullshit, balderdash, poppycock etc.

Granville Books
via email

comely

Comely – a lovely word to describe a woman of more than pencil thin proportions.

Mariella Frostrup
(television presenter)

communion

Communion. It embraces ideas like community and the sexual union. I love the service too.

Peter Florence
(Artistic Director, The Word)

compassion

My favourite word would be compassion. No explanations necessary I hope.

Adrian Noble
(Artistic Director, Royal
Shakespeare Company)

controversy

My favourite word is controversy because it can be pronounced 4 different ways!

Charmaine Bourton
Croydon

controversy

My favourite word is controversy because it causes such controversy in our household over the pronunciation.

Carol Upton
via email

Daddy

Daddy. This is my favourite word because I love my Dad and it reminds me of him even though he is in a better place with God. It has a soft dreamy sound. It suggests love, happiness and care.

Priya C. Mistry, age 10
St Matthews Bloxam School
Rugby

darling

My favourite word is Darling because I can never remember people's names when I'm introduced to them at big functions.

Barbara Windsor
(actress)

dog

My favourite word is dog. It was
about the fourth word I learnt.
It's easy to spell and easy to
remember. It comes from the old
English 'docga' and can, of
course, also be a verb, though no
one told me that for a long time.
Look a dog in the eye and shout
'Dog' and it will certainly lick
you or bite your nose or roll on
its back, grinning. This proves that
the old English knew what they
were doing. The French got it
hopelessly wrong with '*chien*'. The
Spanish did better with '*perro*'.
The German '*hund*' is good. But
'dog' is the word the animals
would have chosen for
themselves.

Andrew Miller
(author)

elbow

My favourite word is elbow not for its meaning but for the way it feels when you say it.

Interestingly, it was one of two words that Michael Gambon said were his favourite words in the Singing Detective – August and elbow.

Nicola Mills
via email

elbow *n.* **JOINT IN THE ARM** the joint between the upper and lower parts of the human arm *vti.* **PUSH STH WITH THE ELBOW** to push or hit sb or sth with the elbow, or progress through a crowd by pushing with the elbow or elbows [Old English *el(n)boga.*]

(ENCARTA WORLD ENGLISH DICTIONARY)

eleemosynary

I am choosing the word eleemosynary because it is so strange and exotic and unfamiliar that one wonders what it is doing in the language at all. But it has a perfectly good function, to describe, in one word, anything 'relating to charity or almsgiving'. So, it is highly relevant, is eccentric, and its agreeable whiff of Greek Orthodox monasteries demonstrates how adept the English have been in borrowing from other languages to create their own.

Michael Palin
(writer and actor)

energy

My favourite word is energy, and my reason is as follows:

*'Energy plus talent, you're a king
Energy plus no talent, you're a
    prince
Talent and no energy, you're a
    pauper.'*

Jeffrey Archer
(author and politician)

epitome

My favourite word is epitome. Why? Because I love that it's the thing that sums everything up. And because I disgraced myself as an English undergraduate by pronouncing it phonetically, with three syllables.

Adrienne Skelton
via email

Everest

Everest is my favourite word. We all have our Everests, whether it's achieving some ambition or telling an uncle you've not spoken to in 30 years, 'I love you.'

Brian Blessed
(actor and adventurer)

existentialist

I first heard the word existentialist at a party when I was 18 and loved it so much that I tried to bring it into every conversation I had. It rolls off the tongue beautifully and I loved saying it, especially when I found out the meaning of it. It's been a favourite word ever since and I am now 63.

Caroline Sinclair
Sunbury

fabulous

Tina Arena
(singer)

fabulous *adj.* **1. EXCELLENT** extremely good, pleasant, or enjoyable (*informal*) **2. AMAZING** amazingly or almost unbelievably great or wonderful **3. TYPICAL OF A FABLE** existing only in, described in, or typical of myths and legends [15thC. Directly or via French *fabuleux* from Latin *fabulosus*.]

(ENCARTA WORLD ENGLISH DICTIONARY)

facetious

Facetious. It is the only word in the English language that uses all the vowels in order.

J.L. Beauchamp
Salisbury

facetious *adj.* **1. SUPPOSED TO BE FUNNY** intended to be humorous but often silly or inappropriate **2. NOT IN EARNEST** not to be taken seriously [Late 16thC. From French *facétieux*, from *facétie* 'joke', from Latin *facetus* 'graceful, witty'.]

(ENCARTA WORLD ENGLISH DICTIONARY)

facilitate

When writing to submit a favourite word, I need to know what would best facilitate the essence of that which I wish to convey in order to facilitate the object of the exercise. 'Non-verbal Linguisthetics' is three words, so I guess to facilitate matters, I'll stick with facilitate, thanks.

Hazel Speed
via email

fish

Fish: Because I am a vegetarian.

Spike Milligan
(actor and author)

flibbertigibbet

Steven Appleby
(author)

flibbertigibbet *n.* a silly, irresponsible, or scatterbrained person, especially one who prattles or gossips (*dated*) [15thC. Origin uncertain: probably an imitation of the sound of meaningless prattle.]
(ENCARTA WORLD ENGLISH DICTIONARY)

floccinaucinihilipilification

My favourite word is floccinaucinihilipilification – and do I really have to have a reason? Because it is fun! I can spell it with my eyes closed…always a good party trick.

Jessica Rovay
San Jose, CA, via email

gazebo

My favourite word is gazebo. I don't know why. It's just one of those words that get funnier and funnier every time you say it. Go on, give it a try. Say it in your head over and over again. I guarantee you'll give a little chuckle to yourself.

James Moores, age 14
Taunton

giggle

Giggle has got to be my favourite word.

Zinnia Butterfield
via email

ginnel

Ginnel. It's a word that sounds like what it is, that evokes a whole world, and so, for me, is a kind of talisman too.

Bill Swainson
(Chair, The Word)

gnarled

Gnarled because it sounds so good and has got that 'g' at the front.

Tony Robinson
(actor and writer)

gnarled *adj.* **1. KNOTTED AND TWISTED** twisted and full of knots **2. TWISTED, MISSHAPEN, OR WEATHER-BEATEN** twisted, misshapen, or weather-beaten because of age, hard work, or illness [Early 17thC. Alteration of *knurled*.]
(ENCARTA WORLD ENGLISH DICTIONARY)

gonzo

Gonzo – a word coined by Bill Cardoso to describe a new journalistic genre in which the instigators of the 'journalism' become an integral part of the story being covered. Kentucky Derby 1970 was the first example to attract world attention (see *The New Journalism* by Tom Wolfe). Gutterel is a language spoken by those whose tongues have come adrift from the stylomandibular ligaments in the mouth causing uncontrolled mandibular oscillations from the victim. Gibberish also falls into this category except that the speaker's use of it is driven by stupidity and a helpless lack of self-control as practised by our current crop of politicians. Entwangled – an invented word combining 'entangled' and 'entwined' which suggests an amorous embrace between octopuses.

Ralph Steadman
(cartoonist, illustrator and writer)

gorgeous

Julia Carling
(television presenter)

gorgeous *adj.* **1. BEAUTIFUL**
outstandingly beautiful or richly
coloured **2. PLEASING** very pleasant
(*informal*) [15thC. From Old French
gorgias 'stylish, elegant', of uncertain origin.]
(ENCARTA WORLD ENGLISH DICTIONARY)

grace

Grace: it embodies everything I
think is elegant and fine about
life. I think people without grace
are pretty unspeakable.

Sir Trevor McDonald
(newscaster)

halcyon

My favourite word is halcyon –
the old word for kingfisher. Not
only does it evoke memories of
this brightly coloured little bird
but also of long sunny days spent
along country riverbanks
enjoying the weather and
watching the wildlife. As as added
benefit, the word itself also has a
lyrical ring to it.

Maria Rookyard

happiness

Happiness because, as I often
sing, 'I thank the Lord that I've
been blessed with more than my
fair share'.

Ken Dodd
(comedian)

happiness

Paul Smith
(clothes designer)

harmony

I imagine everyone will say how impossible it is to choose one word. It is hard. I was going to choose 'music' but instead I will choose harmony. Harmony implies the balancing of different voices to produce a state that can been deeply satisfying. Our world always has needed and always will need harmony and I nominate it as my selected word.

Terry Waite CBE
(author and broadcaster)

hedgehog

My favourite word in English is hedgehog. It sounds so nice when pronounced correctly and it's also quite amusing when little children are learning animal names and hedgehog is often pronounced 'hodgeheg'.

Kirsi-Marja Huhtala
Finland, via email

Hi ho!

Hi ho! Gee, I've said that since I was a tadpole. It's just kind of a friendly welcome that means 'Hi, how are you? I'm glad you're my friend … and for the life of me I can't remember your name.'

Kermit the Frog
(frog and master of ceremonies,
The Muppets)

hiraeth

Hiraeth (Welsh for 'longing for home')

Matthew Rhys
(actor)

holiday

Holiday – because I never seem to get one.

Kerry Hood
via email

holiday *n.* **1. DAY OF LEISURE** a day taken off or set aside for leisure and enjoyment, when sb is exempt from work or normal activity **2. PERIOD OF LEISURE** a period of time free from work or normal activity and given over to leisure and recreation [Old English *haligdaeg.*]

(ENCARTA WORLD ENGLISH DICTIONARY)

holiday

Holiday – because my whole life revolves around work so my main focus in life is getting a break.

Chris Tarrant
(DJ and television presenter)

holiday

Holiday – because it is a much better word than work.

Paul Williams
via email

holiday

Holiday – the reason I live and work …

Julia Hutton
via email

hope

My favourite word is hope,
because you can have nothing
but still have hope.

Cheryl Buxton

via email

hope *vti.* **WANT OR EXPECT STH** to have a
wish to have or do sth or for sth to
happen or be true *n.* **CONFIDENT DESIRE** a
feeling that sth desirable is likely to
happen [Old English *hopian* 'to hope' and
hopa 'hope', of uncertain origin.]

(ENCARTA WORLD ENGLISH DICTIONARY)

I

The naked affirmation of
individuality

Antoinet Berry

via email

ineluctable

Five years ago I was living in
Mauritius and one day while I
was enjoying a post-prandial
siesta with my cat, Josser, my wife
came upon us and growled: 'Are
you going to do any work?'
Without opening my eyes, I
replied, ever so gently: 'Darling,
my ineluctable devotion to your
loveliness is my life's work.'
Whereupon, she slung an over-
ripe mango at my left ear. She
missed and the mango hit me
plum in the mouth and exploded
all over my multi-coloured 'Stay
Cool' T-shirt. Josser, my beloved
cat, got such a fright that she
disappeared for three hours. My
favourite word is ineluctable.

Joe Donovan
via email

ingenious

My favourite word is ingenious –
because it captures that
technical, gritty sense intrinsic to
originality, and which has made
ingenuity, since the seventeenth
century, the most crucial type of
inventive creativity.

Lisa Jardine
via email

inkling

I have chosen the word inkling as
it sounds so 'English'. It was used
by Dame Elizabeth Taylor as she
was photographed outside
Buckingham Palace on the day
she was invested by the Queen.
Dame Elizabeth said she had 'no
inkling' she was to become a
dame. I loved her use of the
word.

M. Coupe
Bolsover

kids

kids

Kids – mine … I think about
them all the time. I worry about
them, they bring me real joy, they
bring me absolute happiness,
they keep my life in perspective,
and they keep me young!

Brian Maclaurin

kid *n.* **1. CHILD** a young child (*informal*)
2. YOUNG GOAT a young goat, antelope,
or similar animal **3. YOUTH** a young
person (*informal*) **4. SOFT LEATHER** soft
leather made from the skin of a young
goat **5. US TERM OF ADDRESS** used as an
informal term of address (*informal*)
[12thC. From Old Norse *kio.*]

(ENCARTA WORLD ENGLISH DICTIONARY)

laconic

Currently my favourite word is laconic, although it's not a word you can easily slip into small talk. It's an adjective that derives from the Greek that originally described the people of Sparta who were famously taciturn and given to short, pithy phrases. Cocktail banter was not big in Sparta. The Duke of Wellington was also a celebrated laconic (can I use it as a noun?). When asked by his local vicar what he would like Sunday's sermon to be about ... he replied, 'about five minutes!' Now that's what I call laconic.

Sting
(musician)

lemur

Lemur is a fantastic word. It's elongated at the beginning and kinda drops off at the end ... lovely. It has a prehensile tail, too, which is just cool. (Can this be a half-vote for prehensile? That's a good one as well.)

Tricia Ellis
via email

lemur *n.* a primate with a long snout, large ears, and a long tail, found only in Madagascar and nearby islands. Family: Lemuridae. [Late 18thC. Via modern Latin from Latin *lemures*, because it is nocturnal.]

(ENCARTA WORLD ENGLISH DICTIONARY)

licentious

I write to submit my nomination for the definitive words of today's catalogue. Licentious. A gorgeous word, rich in texture, sensuous in assent, yet laden with larceny. Pleasing, to my mind, at least, typographically, it seduces me into an ideal of non-jealous, non-possessive, 'higher' love. But, in fact, tells of a hedonistic, moral bankruptcy. If any word describes the way our media draws folk into the notion that one can have it all with the cherry on the top, this is it. Not to mention the modern philosophies which promise to deliver material happiness and spiritual fulfilment. I don't want to sound pious — I live by the bloody word. And if I had the money I would go out tomorrow, buy a spanking new sailboat, call her 'Licentious' and

invite lover after lover on board,
to tell them they were my sun,
my moon and my stars. Just to
find out what would happen to
the unpure of heart when they
dished out the goodies on
judgement day. I still haven't
decided yet if it is within our
nature or a sin to be immoral in
love, but I know it is an all-
consuming experiment.

Francis Power
via email

little

My word is little.
As for the reason I chose it – I
don't know why

Sue Townsend
(author)

lovie

My favourite word is Lovie. I call my husband that after 25 years of marriage. It's become more frequent over the years; it's Lovie this, Lovie that, an endearment for the man in my life who grows more dear to me with each passing day. His real name is Jim.

Edith McLaren
Inverurie

love

I consider love to be the most poignant word because it is multifaceted and represents the best in a human being, while its absence dehumanises us. Every person is shaped by love or lack of love in his/her life. Love is the most talked and written about subject in the world.

Efrosyni Hobbs
Plumstead

love

My word is love.
It can convey so many different
aspects of life:
The love you have for your
partner
The love you have for your
children
To make love – where there may
be no love at all
The love God has for us
The love of inanimate objects – I
love Italian food
Etc.

Stephen Rae
via email

lovely

My favourite word is lovely. I am
a primary teacher and I tend to
overuse it when responding to
children's work!

Tony Winfield
via email

47

luscious

Luscious as my fiancé calls me
this every day! And it sounds
better than delicious.

Julia Hamilton
Dumfries

magical

Magical is my favourite word. It
suggests joy and happiness and
fairy tales with mystical knights
and enchanted castles with high
turrets. It also suggests to me an
imaginary place nobody but I can
find.

Samantha Malt, age 11
St Matthews Bloxham School,
Rugby

malacologist

My favourite word is malacologist: a student of molluscs, which is what I was myself for some thirty years. My attachment to the term is increased by the discovery that its root, the Greek 'malakos': soft and floppy, is utilised in Greece as the term for a self-abuser – so much more elegant than the equivalent English word (which is what many of my colleagues use to describe me now that I have taken up publicising science rather than doing it). Another favourite word is mandolinist; which fits me as I used to play that very instrument (but I hesitate to say what it means in French).

Steve Jones
(writer and Professor of
Genetics, University College
London))

melancholy

My favourite word in the
language is melancholy. It has
something wonderfully
Elizabethan about it, and like all
the best words, suggests its
meaning in the way it sounds.
When feeling down, it's so much
better to say, 'Today I'm feeling
melancholy,' rather than simply
depressed or sad; the word is
vague, poetic and full of longing.

Alain de Botton
(writer)

melancholy *adj.* FEELING OR CAUSING
PENSIVE SADNESS feeling or making sb
feel a thoughtful or gentle sadness *n.*
PENSIVE SADNESS thoughtful or gentle
sadness [14thC. Directly or via French
mélancholie from late Latin *melancholia*,
from Greek *melankholia*, literally 'black
bile'.]

(ENCARTA WORLD ENGLISH DICTIONARY)

memories

My favourite word is memories. We all have them and they become precious as we get older. Having recently lost a dear one, just before our Ruby Wedding, I couldn't go on were it not for my memories.

Anon
Bournemouth

mendacious

My favourite word is mendacious. It flows delightfully off the tongue and it was the first word my son learned that made him realise that it was useful to study Latin, because he could work out what the word meant from its Latin root.

Jenni Murray
(broadcaster)

minimum

Minimum because when I used to be a typist (secretary) it was a word which flowed quickly and easily off the typewriter, as well as off the tongue!

Maura Dziuba
Nottingham

moi

Moi is the favourite word of moi because it refers to moi's favourite person: moi. What's not to love?

Miss Piggy
(megastar)

mollycoddle

My favourite word is
mollycoddle. It is one of those
words which sounds best when
spoken and contains many of the
nicest sounds your mouth can
make. 'Cinnamon' is quite good
too as it rolls off the tongue
nicely.
Word are best if they sound
good regardless of meaning.

Katharine Clifton
via email

Montparnasse

Alex James
(bass player – Blur)

53

moonset

moonset

Moonset because it is a nice word to say and is a nice word to contemplate. While everyone uses the word sunset, moonset has a tranquillity and a peacefulness about it which I like.

Richard Whiteley
(quiz show presenter)

moral

My word is moral because I
believe the moral debate is vital,
because people tend to think of
advantage, or effectiveness, as
criteria for decision making
rather than working from first
principles; because having a
moral standpoint is better than
being media driven; because
concepts of right and wrong may
not always be shared, but having
a moral framework makes it
easier to debate the issues.

Rabbi Julia Neuberger
(writer and broadcaster)

mushroom

Mushroom because it's the first word I ever said. I'm very fond of them. I'm not a good cook but I make a wicked mushroom soup.

Baroness Tessa Blackstone
(education minister)

nausea

Will Self
(author)

nausea *n.* 1. SICKNESS OF THE STOMACH the unsettling feeling in the stomach that accompanies the urge to vomit 2. DISGUST deep disgust (*literary*) [15thC. Via Latin and Greek *nausia* from, ultimately, *naus* (see NAUTICAL). The underlying idea is of seasickness.]

(ENCARTA WORLD ENGLISH DICTIONARY)

nightmare

It's hard to pick one favourite word, but in the running are truffle, pooch, plashing, cthonic, and nightmare. Nightmare is one of those beautiful (sounding) words with an unfortunate association. There are also a bouquet of flowers whose names I adore: violet, peony, anemone, and wisteria, although the French for wisteria is much more beautiful: *glycine*. Also in French I have always loved *parapluie*, though I suppose that can't count. What fun! Love, Judith

Judith Thurman
(author)

nipples

Nipples: A word that perfectly matches what it describes: slightly silly, but potent. Imagine how much of their power nipples would lose if they were called something plain like 'arms' or 'tables'.

Simon Nye
(writer of *Men Behaving Badly*)

nostalgia

Nostalgia is a lovely, gentle-sounding word and I also love what it represents – countless memories of laughter and adventure.

Max Clifford
(publicist)

not guilty

My selection is, unfortunately, two words, as originally nominated by Mark Twain: not guilty.

E.K. Morrison
Weston-super-Mare

numismatist

One of my favourite words is numismatist – nothing to do with the meaning, just the sound it makes when you say it slowly.

Edwin Hird
via email

numpty

Numpty: It sounds like and conjures up exactly the meaning it is meant to convey: a numskull, nincompoop, ninny.

Andrew Neil
(editor, writer and broadcaster)

obviously

Obviously 'obviously' is Britain's favourite word.

Pat Arrowsmith
London

onomatopoeia

My favourite word is onomatopoeia, because I like the sound of it; I love the sounds of words, and this word is about the sounds that words make.

Dame Judi Dench, DBE
(actress)

opsimath

Opsimath means a person who learns late in life, which I think sums me up.

Magnus Magnusson
(writer and broadcaster)

Palestine

I have for long loved the word Palestine. Apart from its lovely sound, it conjures up so many pleasant pictures in my mind – especially my remembrance of passing through it one Sunday en route to Lebanon during the Second World War and savouring the heady aroma of orange and lemon groves.

Richard Ridyard
Rotherham

parabolic

Parabolic: ever since the *Observer* TV correspondent, reviewing the Miss World competition years ago, described one participant as 'parabolic Miss Venezuela' I have fantasised about her beauty. Never saw the woman, but who needs to when one has such an incredibly sexy adjective? Beauty is skin deep. Words are forever.

David Newby
Graz, Austria, via email

parents

Parents Why? The word 'parents' reminds me of my mum and dad and it means I have someone to love. I will always remember the word 'parents' because they are always there for me.

David Simpson

peaceful

I nominate peaceful because
1 Everyone knows it
2 It has a restful sound
3 It is the very opposite of stressful
4 Anything to do with peace is desirable

Stanley Shoop
Elstree

Peep peep!

Peep peep! – because that's how
I say hello to all my friends.

Thomas the Tank Engine

peony

My favourite word is peony – I'm
not sure if I'm spelling it right – a
name of a flower, an early
blossomer. My favourite comes in
hues of dark blood-red and the
petals last for an all-too-brief
time. For this gorgeous sounding
word and its little time in bloom
I choose it. Next was crumpet –
there's so many.

Cerys Matthews
(singer – Catatonia)

peripatetic

I've always liked peripatetic – it just sounds right when walking around.

John Kelland
via email

petition

My favourite word is petition, used as a verb.

Ian McKillop
(author)

plinth

Stephen Fry
(writer and actor)

prat

My word is prat. It describes a
person so magnificently,
especially the prat who thought
up this stupid competition. And
me for entering it!

F. Frost
West Dulwich

procrastinate

Procrastinate is my favourite
word, Why? Because it's a word
my partner has used since the
onset of our relationship. 'Don't
procrastinate', he says whenever
I say I don't want to do
something. If a week goes by
when he hasn't used it, I start to
worry!

Deana Emment

prodigious

For years my favourite word was prodigious. Gabriel García Márquez, who is one of my heroes, uses it a lot, and I have acquired the habit from him. It's equally good in French and Spanish, which is a bonus. I don't seem to have favourite word at the moment, but before 'prodigious' it was exiguous which I first fell in love with in a Nicholas Monsarrat novel.

Louis de Bernières
(author)

prodigious *adj.* **1.** SIZABLE great in amount, size, or extent **2.** MARVELLOUS very impressive or amazing [Mid-16thC. From Latin *prodigiosus* 'marvellous'.]
(ENCARTA WORLD ENGLISH DICTIONARY)

prudent

Prudent because a prudent person is someone who is careful and it's on my key ring. Also I like saying it to people who drop or break things, especially my sister, who breaks everything in the house.

Chaz Plummer
Mill Vale Middle School,
Dunstable

pure

Pure, because in this polluted atmosphere it brings the vision of a clean, beautiful and natural world. It suggests a clear sky and clean water of the fountains.

Michael Jones, age 11
St Matthews Bloxam school,
Rugby

quetzal

My favourite word is Quetzal
which is very useful when playing
Scrabble.

Robert Hammond-Smith
via email

quidditch

My favourite word is quidditch. It
comes from my favourite book
and it is such a simple word, but
is so difficult to explain. It is also
magical which makes me feel
quite good.

Stewart Farmer, age 14
(*Harry Potter* fan)

refuge

Erin Pizzey
(founder of Shelter)

rickshaw

Rickshaw because it has a lot of history in its Japanese/Indian roots. It describes a vehicle that's a monument to man's ingenuity and for the last seven years I've been doing my bit to re-introduce it to the UK traffic mix!

Erica Steinhaner
(British Rickshaw Network)
Oxford

rock 'n' roll

Rock 'n' roll is the most important word I know and one of the great slang words. It rolls off the tongue and its strength is that it is dismissed by those who don't understand it and is superbly meaningful to those who do.

Julian Cope
(musician)

rotund

One of my favourite words is rotund – a precise but affectionate adjective

Sue Lawley
(broadcaster)

sandwich

Sandwich has always been a favourite; probably because when learning to read and having to break words down into their phonetic components I stood at the side of the teacher's desk, reading out a Janet and John story. When I got to this strange new (long!) word, I broke it down into its respective parts and immediately had a picture of a witch's hat on a beach – I thought the word meant a 'Sand Witch'. Similarly psychotherapist: when first I came across that particular word, I read it as 'Psycho The Rapist.' So, just two of many thousands of favourites.

Willy Russell
(playwright)

satisfactory

Satisfactory because it shows
things are just as they should be.

Patrick Moore
(astronomer, author and
broadcaster)

sensual

My favourite word is sensual.

Carole Blake
(literary agent)

sensuous

Lisa l'Anson
(Radio One DJ)

sensuous *adj.* **1.** OF SENSE STIMULATION
relating to stimulation of the senses **2.**
APPRECIATING STIMULATION enjoying or
appreciating pleasurable stimulation
of the senses **3.** CAUSING STIMULATION
causing pleasurable stimulation of the
senses [Mid-17thC. Coined from Latin
sensus.]

(ENCARTA WORLD ENGLISH DICTIONARY)

serendipity

Serendipity is a lovely-sounding
word whose meaning keeps my
hopes alive that my fortunes in
all respects will suddenly, out of
the blue, improve.

G. Barrett
Bury

serendipity

Serendipity, the faculty of making happy, chance finds has a wonderful, jaunty ring to it; it also trips off the tongue beautifully. Life is full of happy, unexpected surprises and discoveries (like finding a lost and loved teddy bear when hunting for an important file). It signals hope and joy and reminds us that not all accidents are unwelcome, unhappy or damaging – as with the discovery of Serendip, from which the word originates. NB Serendip was the previous name for Ceylon, now Sri Lanka.

A. Bartlett
Shepton Mallet

serendipity

Whether serendipity is chance
or divine providence – and I
prefer to think it is the latter –
nevertheless when things get
tough, it is always sent.

Jonathan Sacks
(Chief Rabbi)

serendipity

Serendipity. Why? Well, just say it
and feel your tongue travel
round your mouth, then your lips
come together – very satisfying,
physically. And, intellectually, it is
open-ended, suggesting a free-
wheeling approach to life itself, a
certain faith in letting nature and
destiny shape our existence,
opening our minds to the new,
the rare, the unusual, the
unexplained.

Maneesha Sharma
Harrow

serenity

Ringo Starr
(drummer – The Beatles)

sesquipedalian

My favourite word is sesquipedalian. I have always liked it since reading Mrs Gaskell's *Cranford*, and I couldn't wait to find the definition of the word in the dictionary.

J. Colloby
Tyldesley

singleton

My favourite word in the English language is singleton. The reason for this is 1) it is replacing the derogative and outdated word 'spinster' with its ridiculous connotations of shelves, spinning wheels, rejection and failure which have nothing to do with the lives of modern single women. 2) Everyone thinks I invented it in *Bridget Jones' Diary*, whereas in fact it was P.G. Wodehouse.

Helen Fielding
(author)

snooze

It's got to be snooze – because snoooze means a few more snuggly minutes in bed on a cold, grey morning, a stolen siesta, daydreams, sex on a sunny afternoon …

Rachel Parsons
via email

squelch

My favourite word is squelch because I like the sound of it.

Dianne Jefferson
Mitcham

sundown

Sundown. Whatever the day has been like, sundown starts to bring it to an end. It also conjures up a picture of the beauty of the sky at twilight.

L. Brookes
Fulwood

sunnies

Danni Minogue
(singer)

sunshine

My favourite word is sunshine. It just brightens your day. It also reminds me of Morcambe and Wise, which can't be bad, can it?

Mavis Parkin
via email

susurration

I like the fortuitous onomatopoeia of words for soundless things. Gleam, glint, glitter, glisten … they all sound exactly as the light would sound if it made a noise. Glint is sharp and quick, it 'glints', and if an oily surface made it noise it would go 'glisten'. And bliss sounds like a cream bun melting. But I'll plump for: susurration … from the Latin '*susurrus*': whisper or rustling, which is exactly what it sounds like. It's a hushed noise. But it hints of plots and secrets and people turning to one another in surprise. It's the noise, in fact, made just after the sword is withdrawn from the stone and just before the cheering starts.

Terry Pratchett
(author)

swanning

Swanning (as in 'swanning off').
This word generates pictures of
family members sliding away to
avoid washing up or my husband
slipping off on a dubious errand,
whilst yet conveying the dignity
the unapproved errand may have
… as white birds gliding down a
willow-shaded river.

Susan Siddeley
via email

sympathy

My favourite word is sympathy,
for both its meaning and its soft
sound when spoken aloud.

Robert Potter
via email

tautology

Tautology: a wonderful sounding word and also underused. Yet people use tautologies every day without realising – PIN number and NCP car park, to illustrate but two. I could probably find more if pushed but it's late and I'm drunk …

Shirley Humphreys
via email

tawny

Russell Hoban
(author)

team

I vote for TEAM because Together Everyone Achieves More.

Pete Harding
via email

tenacious

Tenacious – It's a nice word and most people who have battled and conquered dyslexia have a large amount of tenacity.

Anthea Turner
(television presenter, The Word
supports the British Dyslexia
Association)

thank you

My favourite word is thank you because it's worth saying just to see someone smile. I use it quite a lot.

P. Allan
Kings Langley

ticketyboo

Ticketyboo … my father used to
say this when everything was
OK.
(Also, gorgeous … this used to
roll off my stepfather's Scottish
tongue beautifully and it related
to anything from flowers and
babies to food.)

Mary Brown
via email

tintinnabulation

I have always been fond of
Tintinnabulation but to be
honest the one that really lifts
my spirit is Caipirinha? …
Brazilian nectar of the gods …
but are foreign words allowed?

Liz Calder
(publisher)

tmesis

Serendipity and quidditch?
Second-rate, uninspiring claptrap.
I demand a recount. What is the
basis of your voting structure?
Do you have a panel? Are they
women? I implore you to
reconsider the merits of tmesis:
succinct, poignant, with literally
hundreds of practical uses.
Fanbloodytastic!

Kester Peters
via email

tmesis

Tmesis – because it's fan-bloody-
tastic and the only word to begin
'tm' and because the word itself
can be said in emphatic tones.

Penny Quayle
via email

together

TOGETHER because when together, human beings are at their fullest.

Chris Smith
(Secretary of State for Culture,
Media and Sport)

tomorrow

My favourite word is TOMORROW - a word full of hope, promise and the yearning for a brighter day, a word that can always give your sagging spirit a life, a word that is never out of style, a word that contains the best of us.

Tony Parsons
(author)

tranquillity

My favourite word would have to be tranquillity. It's just a word that makes me think of a quiet beach where all you can hear is the sound of the birds and the waves.

Ronnie Freer
via email

twelve

TWELVE: for the melancholy beauty of its sound.

Carol Anne Duffy
(poet)

um

My nomination for a favourite word is um. This seems to be the most often used word but is not in any dictionary!!

Ken Robinson
via email

weather

My favourite word is weather. It is said at least once a day by everybody! It is used to start a conversation with a stranger and as a way of changing the subject quickly in tricky situations. It must be one of the most popular topics in Britain.

Franca Gatto
via email

whatever

My favourite word is whatever. I like it becaue you can say it in so many ways and it just sounds so cool.

Claire MacGillivray
via email

whimsy

WHIMSY. It is almost onomatopoeic, floating light as a feather across the page, defying rationality and basking in self-indulgence.

Max Hastings
(editor, *The Evening Standard*)

widdershins

Widdershins: Fabulous alternative word for 'anticlockwise', as it must pre-date the invention of clocks and, therefore, takes one straight into some medieval world where the sun, moon and seasons used to rule the pattern of our daily life. It also sounds glorious, more like music than a word.

Michael Tame
via email

wonder

Ian Rickson
(Director – The Royal Court
Theatre)

wonder *n.* AMAZED ADMIRATION amazed admiration or awe, especially at sth very beautiful or new *vti.* SPECULATE ABOUT STH to speculate or be curious to know about sth *vi* BE AMAZED to be in a state of amazed admiration or awe [Old English *wundor,* from a prehistoric Germanic word.]

(ENCARTA WORLD ENGLISH DICTIONARY)

wonderful

My favourite word is wonderful
– a lovely, positive adjective
which is not over-used like
'fabulous', yet suggests
excitement and excellence.

Gill Michelmore
Snettisham

yes

Justine Frischmann
(musician – Elastica)

you

You. It makes such a pleasant
contrast to the continuous 'I' and
'Me' that you hear far too much
of these days.

Alan Ayckbourn
via email

zucchini

Zucchini – it makes me laugh
and feel happy.

Darren Lumber, age 15
Taunton

Encarta® Book of Quotations

Ed. Bill Swainson

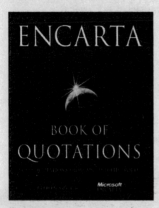

The most international and contemporary collection of quotations – more than half since 1900 – from Einstein to The Simpsons

'A quotation at the right moment is like bread to the famished.'
The Talmud

- 25,000 quotations by more than 6,200 authors
- More than 5,000 new quotations on science, technology, communication, business, medicine, psychology, the arts and popular culture
- Includes some of the first sayings of the 21st century
- More than 1,000 quotations by the famous on the famous or infamous and vice versa – from Cicero on Socrates to Gore Vidal on Andy Warhol
- 5,000 more quotations and 3,500 more contributors than any other dictionary of quotations currently available

£30

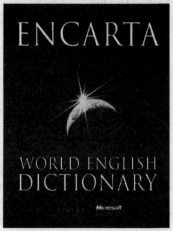

WIN £1,000!

Use the five words below in a piece of writing
containing no more than fifty words and win £1,000
for the charity of your choice.

Serendipity
Quidditch
Love
Peace
Onomatopoeia

Send your entry to: The Book of Favourite Words
competition, Bloomsbury Publishing Plc, 38 Soho
Square, London W1D 3HB

• All entries must be no more than fifty words in length.
• The entrant's name and address must be clearly marked
at the top of each entry.
• The judges' decision is final and no correspondence will
be entered into concerning the result.
• If you wish your entry to be returned it must be
accompanied by a stamped, addressed envelope.
• The competition is not open to employees of
Bloomsbury Publishing or The Word festival.
• The closing date for entries is 1st May 2001. No entries
will be accepted after that date.